READY.
SET.
NEXT.

THE JOURNEY AFTER HIGH SCHOOL

BY CHUCK BOMAR

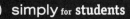
simply for students

Ready. Set. Next.
The Journey After High School

© 2014 Chuck Bomar   0000 0000 6116 259X

group.com
simplyyouthministry.com

Credits
Author: Chuck Bomar
Executive Developer: Jason Ostrander
Chief Creative Officer: Joani Schultz
Editor: Rob Cunningham
Cover Art: Amy Hood, from Hoodzpah Design
Art Director & Production: Veronica Preston

Scripture quotations are from The Holy Bible, English Standard Version® (ESV®), copyright © 2001 by Crossway, a publishing ministry of Good News Publishers. Used by permission. All rights reserved.

ISBN 978-1-4707-1356-0

10 9 8 7 6 5 4 3 2   20 19 18 17

Printed in the United States of America.

DEDICATION

This book is dedicated to everyone who is open to being who God has called them to be.

TABLE OF CONTENTS

READY. SET. NEXT.

START HERE

AN INTRODUCTION

You have a lot to think about right now.
But this book wasn't written to give you a bunch of information.

This book is about helping you think, for yourself.
This book is about following the journey of a few people who are in the same season of life that you're in right now.

John, Amy, and Chloe—all three of them, like you, are at a pivotal point of life.
It's a sort of fork in the road for them.
This is where life directions are chosen and lessons are learned.

Whether or not you feel ready for this next phase of life, there are likely a lot of things you have yet to think through. That's why getting a glimpse into the lives and struggles and questions of John, Amy, and Chloe can be helpful.

You will identify with certain parts of their lives.
And you will likely find things in their stories that are different from you.
But I believe you can learn from both sides of that fence.

Nobody has all this figured out, so I'm sure you have hesitations and concerns about life after high school, much like the characters

in the following pages have.
But there is much to be excited about.
And even more to process through.

Life is about to surprise you in many ways. Some things you will definitely enjoy—and others will shockingly slap you in the face.

But this book isn't filled with a bunch of do's and don'ts for you to follow.
This is just a look into the journey of three people in their first few years after high school.

My hope is that this book helps you think, perhaps a little differently and more intentionally, about a few areas of your life.

I'll first introduce you to John...

CHAPTER 1

THERE'S A LOT TO THINK ABOUT

PROFILE: JOHN

Age: 17

Year: High school senior

Sport: Baseball

Parents: Divorced

Car: 1978 BMW 320i

Genre of music: Pretty much anything but country

Paused on iTunes: Drake—"Hold On, We're Going Home"

Quirk: Genius thing with math

Wants to: Own his own business

Pet peeve: Getting his socks wet

THERE'S A LOT TO THINK ABOUT

John and Stephan didn't always get along when they were younger, but these days John loves talking with his big brother. Stephan is such a perfect sounding board. He lives a few hours away from the family, and he has a solid idea of what John's about to face because he's gone through a bunch of his own big transitions in life—some smooth, many rocky.

It's not like graduating from high school will be John's first big transition. His parents divorced when he was 8. That was rough. He lives with his mom, but he still spends a lot of time with his dad. Things are better than they used to be. But his life is far from perfect.

John respects his parents—a lot. He knows they love him and want the best for him, but they keep asking him a ton of questions he can't answer yet. Both his mom and dad want him to go to a "good school," but he isn't convinced. In fact, he thinks it's kind of a waste of money at this point. He doesn't even know what he wants to do with his life yet. His girlfriend's parents seem to be a lot more chill about this whole college thing than his parents are. And her parents seem to have a much more practical view of how much money it would cost.

Ahh yes, his girlfriend. John's a popular guy at school, with a lot of friends, and everyone likes him—but especially Sasha, who's also a senior. They've been dating for about seven months, and each week he seems to learn something new about how their families are so, well, *different* from each other.

Sasha's parents seem to be handling everything so much better—and that gets John even more annoyed with *his* parents. It's super frustrating, but he can't really talk to them about what he wants to do after high school because it always seems to turn into an argument. They just keep reminding him of all the things he is *not* doing—all the stuff he still has to finish before graduation.

John finds himself just wanting to be on his own. He feels like he needs some space. More freedom would be nice.

It's not that John doesn't understand that a lot of things in his life are about to change. He gets it, and he *is* excited for the change. It just seems like his parents don't think he realizes *just how much* things are gonna change.

This all came to the surface one morning last week. John was sitting at the island in the kitchen, eating a bowl of Lucky Charms. His mom walked in, poured coffee into her favorite mug, leaned against the island, looked him straight in the eye, and asked, "Are you doing OK?"

"Yeah, I'm fine," John replied. He wanted to say, "Don't interrogate me like I've just been arrested." But he didn't.

His mom poured French Vanilla creamer into her coffee. John wasn't convinced she believed that he really was fine.

"Hey, I was thinking," she said. "Maybe tonight we could look over some of the dorm orientation stuff together."

THERE'S A LOT TO THINK ABOUT

"I'd rather not," John said. He couldn't hide his obvious frustration. Discussing dorm orientation stuff with his mom sounded as fun as pulling out a fingernail with a pair of pliers. Well, not really, but it *was* just about the last thing he wanted to do—especially after a full day of school and then baseball practice.

"Well, you may not want to," she said, "but you should know what's going on. I mean, do you know what the meal plan is like, or what you're supposed to do before you move in, or how they choose your roommate?"

"No. And, truthfully, Mom, I don't really care right now."

"I think you should care. There's a lot to think about. Well, just know that I'd like to talk about it tonight, OK?"

"Sure," John mumbled as he got up and walked over to the sink.

This wasn't a new discussion. It seemed like John was having this kind of conversation all the time with each parent. They kept getting on him over every little detail about what he was going to do in a few months. He just figured everything would work itself out. From his perspective, his parents were freaking out. Because that's what parents do, right?

John went to school and then baseball practice. When he got home, he grabbed four Oreo cookies from the pantry and headed to his room. He opened his laptop and scrolled through Facebook to see what all his friends were up to. One particular post caught his eye, from a friend who graduated from his school a year earlier. As John read it, he started to get a little overwhelmed...

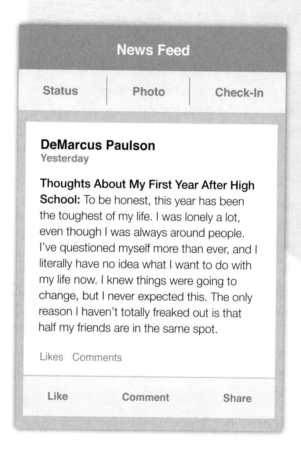

News Feed

| Status | Photo | Check-In |

DeMarcus Paulson
Yesterday

Thoughts About My First Year After High School: To be honest, this year has been the toughest of my life. I was lonely a lot, even though I was always around people. I've questioned myself more than ever, and I literally have no idea what I want to do with my life now. I knew things were going to change, but I never expected this. The only reason I haven't totally freaked out is that half my friends are in the same spot.

Likes Comments

Like   Comment   Share

THERE'S A LOT TO THINK ABOUT

Suddenly and unexpectedly, John got even more nervous. He opened another tab in his browser and searched for "Stress in college students." He didn't immediately click on any of the links. He didn't have to. Just seeing the summaries for the endless list of links was totally overwhelming. He decided to check out some of the links, and he quickly realized that stress was a huge issue in college—and for everyone making the jump from high school into a new season of life, whatever path they choose.

He closed the laptop, stood up, and went and plopped down on his bed. All sorts of thoughts crossed through his mind…

What's my roommate going to be like?
Am I gonna lose Sasha by moving to another town?
None of my friends are going to the same school.
I gotta talk to my dad about how we are gonna pay for all this.
Maybe I should get a job.
I'm super bummed I can't take my car as a freshman.

John was beginning to realize that life after high school wasn't going to really be what he thought, hoped, or expected. But did that mean it was something to fear?

READY. SET. NEXT.

Take some time to process through what you envision life after high school will be like for you. Maybe write out your thoughts on a page or two, or summarize things in a few bullet points. You might even want to chart out what you think the schedule for a typical week might look like. Consider the following questions:

1. What are some specific things that excite you about life after high school?

2. What are some specific things about this next season of life that make you a little nervous?

3. What is one specific dream you have about your first year after high school?

4. What are some unanswered questions you have?

5. What do you think will be the biggest, toughest transition you'll face?

CHAPTER 2

CHANGE CAN BE *REALLY* DIFFICULT

PROFILE: AMY

Age: 19

Year: College freshman

Sport: Doesn't like any sports

Parents: Married for 22 years

Car: 2009 Chevy Cavalier

—but it's at her parents' house

Genre of music: Rock, Top 40 stuff

Paused on iTunes: Muse—"Uprising"

Quirk: Has never tried ranch dressing

Wants to: Be herself

Pet peeve: People who always sigh or fake yawn

Amy tends to be a little on the quiet side. She's not really shy, just more reserved. She likes to have a couple of close friends and can be social, but she likes her space, too. It's a little complex, but nothing abnormal. People like her because she's a peaceful person to have around. She has a gentle spirit, she is super nice, and sometimes, when laughing really hard, she snorts a little. It's why her parents nicknamed her "Piglet" when she was younger.

Amy has a great relationship with both of her parents, who've been married for over two decades. She just finished her first semester away at school and really missed them while she was gone. She especially missed home when all the crazy girls were running through the dorm hallways at 2 a.m., screaming at the top of their lungs, "Mighty girls at large." Things like that made her miss the quietness and comfort of her home. She missed the little things: having a home-cooked meal with her parents, watching *Jeopardy* with her dad, and sleeping in the twin bed she's had since she was 5 years old.

Her first semester away was tougher on her than she ever dreamed it would be. It was fun but emotionally tough at times. A journal entry she wrote after being at school for a few weeks expresses it well:

CHANGE CAN BE *REALLY* DIFFICULT

'Lonely even though people are around'

That's how I feel.

I just don't think I handle change as well as I thought I would.

New city. New friends. New routines. No car.

Everyone at school was really nice and wanted to hang out at first. We talked late at night as we sat in the hallway in our pajamas, went to 'the shake shack' at midnight, and did a MASH marathon. I had never heard of that show before, but it was fun to watch an old show like that. But now that classes have started, everyone is heading in different directions. The crazy thing is, I don't think anybody knows where they're headed quite yet. All I know is that people aren't hanging out as much. We're too busy.

I never thought I would say it, but I miss high school. I miss hanging out at the overhang in the quad every morning. I liked who I was in high school. I used to be excited to move on from that, but now I miss it.

Change is hard and all the changes are somehow changing me.

I just don't know how yet.

I'm sure I'll figure it out.

Amy was realizing just how much life changes when things change. The hardest part was trying to figure out who she was in light of all the changes. She liked who she was in high school. She had a set group of friends. She had a routine. She had an "identity" on campus. Some people might have seen a new start at another school as refreshing, but it's been difficult for Amy.

The hardest issue was how all these changes were affecting her personally. In high school she had an identity in her surroundings. But now her surroundings have changed, forcing her to actually figure out who she was apart from all that.

Her family didn't define her anymore. Nobody at college knew who she was.

In high school, the corner of the quad and all the other people who hung out there with her provided a sense of identity. Now there are six quads, a massive student center, four coffee shops within walking distance, and a ton of dorms. Hanging out in just one place doesn't give her an identity with her peers.

She has to figure out who she is as a person. And not only is this a bit of a shock, it's also proving to be difficult. Very difficult.

Amy recently met with her residence hall director for a routine "check-in" every student on the floor has to do. It's just a chance for the RD to meet with each student to go through some rules and guidelines if necessary, but it's mostly just a time to touch base. The RD asked Amy how she was doing—a simple question,

CHANGE CAN BE *REALLY* DIFFICULT

right? But for Amy her response was complex.

"Well, I'm not sure, actually. I'm in a weird place right now." Amy started to tear up. "All my friends are at other schools, so staying in touch is a lot harder than I thought it was going to be. I miss them. I don't really know how I'm doing, but I'm looking forward to seeing my friends during Christmas break. That will be good."

The RD responded, "It's hard when everything changes, huh?"

"Yeah, I guess. I don't know. Maybe I'm just being a baby, but a lot of things are hard right now." Amy paused for a second. "Sheesh, I'm sorry. I don't mean to unload all this on you."

"This is why we have these times, Amy," the RD said graciously.

"Thanks. I guess I didn't realize how much of my life was going to change—and the really weird thing is, I mean, it's like I don't even know who I am anymore." Amy paused for a second and looked at the RD. The RD was so cool. She looked at Amy with the most gracious grin and simply said, "Welcome to college, Amy."

In that moment, Amy knew she wasn't alone. That's when she realized that this was part of life after high school.

Amy left and went for a run. When she got back to the dorm, she began writing a blog post. It's a way she processed through things, but in less intimate ways than her journal.

Change Changes Things

I'm learning a lesson: Change changes things. I'm also realizing that I'm one of the "things" change is changing. And it's not easy. Maybe it's a life lesson everyone needs to learn. Maybe it's part of "growing up."

Nobody talks about it here at school, but about an hour ago I finally had a conversation that gave me some hope that this is normal, that I'm not alone.

But knowing this doesn't help me to not feel overwhelmed. I lost who I was in high school, and I'm trying to figure out who I am now at college, but argh, I just realized that one day I'm going to graduate from college, too—and then what?

Will I have to go through this whole identity crisis all over again?

Yikes!

Maybe the hardest thing to do in life is find out who we are apart from everything and everyone around us. I'm now wondering how to answer a simple question: Who am I?

Comment   Share

READY. SET. NEXT.

Identity is not *an* issue we struggle with after graduating from high school. It's *the* issue. Discovering who we are as individuals may be a little simpler for some people than others, but it's pretty tough for most of us. Consider the following questions:

1. **How would you answer this question: "Who am I?" And how is your answer today different from how you would have answered it a year or two ago?**

2. **What does it mean to think about who you are, apart from your current surroundings?**

3. **What parts of yourself do you never want to change, regardless of where you are or what career path you choose?**

CHAPTER 3

IT'S IMPORTANT TO HAVE A FRAMEWORK

PROFILE: CHLOE

Age: 18

Year: High school senior

Sport: Softball

Parents: Married for 18 years

Car: 1999 Toyota five-speed pickup

Genre of music: Country

Paused on iTunes: Miranda Lambert—"Automatic"

Quirk: Writes in all uppercase letters

Wants to: Stay close to home

Pet peeve: Guys who wear too much cologne

Chloe lives in a small town that's home to just about a thousand people. Her dad owns a small hardware store, and because it's the only one in town, her dad pretty much knows everyone. Chloe has been helping her dad at the store since she was 8 years old. Her mom helps by doing the finances for the store, and she also cuts hair on the side for extra money. The store is a way to make a living, but it's certainly not a way to become wealthy.

Chloe is the oldest of five kids. Her family is very close and Chloe dreams of having a big family of her own one day. The family lives on five acres of land, with a horse, pig, some chickens—and a goat. Nobody knows what the goat is for or why they got it in the first place. All he does is eat grass, but he's part of the family now.

Their property includes a barn, which Chloe loved as a child because her dad transformed the loft into a playroom for her. Her younger siblings use it how, especially her youngest sister, Maria. She's only 4 and loves climbing the ladder that's the only way into the playroom. Other than the playhouse and some bails of alfalfa stacked off to the south side, the barn is filled with antiques her mom and dad collect. Her dad's prize possession is a car from the 1930s, and her mom loves to collect sewing machines.

On one end of the barn is a separate room—perhaps a little odd to have connected to a barn, but it's the room where Chloe's grandmother makes chocolate. She makes all different kinds and sells some, but mostly she just gives the chocolate to people for Christmas or as birthday presents. Chloe loves that her grandma has a hobby. Plus she loves the chocolate and thinks it's a cool family tradition.

After graduating from high school, most kids from her town go to a community college in a city about 20 minutes away. A few kids go farther away to college, but Chloe's parents can't really afford to pay for any college opportunity right now. The hardware store just doesn't make enough money. They've talked about Chloe getting loans, but they don't believe it's wise because they're not sure how she would be able to pay it all back. Chloe is totally fine with that—in fact, she'd rather stay close to home right now and just keep working at her dad's store. She's also thought about getting another job that might make her a little more money—because her dad can't really afford employees.

Chloe has some cousins in Minneapolis who come and visit a couple of times a year. One of them, Jeff, is very ambitious and is going to attend Iowa State to become an engineer. It's an out-of-state school, but he has a full-ride scholarship. Amy and Jeff have always been close, but now she's noticing how their lives seem to be heading in totally different directions. Chloe recently saw something Jeff had posted about college on Facebook:

News Feed

| Status | Photo | Check-In |

Jeff
Yesterday

Excited to get to school and start my life. Iowa State and the engineering world, here I come! #WorldByStorm

Likes Comments

| Like | Comment | Share |

Chloe loves how ambitious Jeff is and hopes the best for him, but she is totally different. Jeff is excited about leaving home, getting his degree, and then starting a career that pays well. He even talks about going to grad school. Chloe, on the other hand, confidently loves being a "small-town girl" and is perfectly content to stick around home. Plus, even if she wanted to leave, she can't afford it. For now she's content working at her dad's store and trying to save up her money.

Chloe's latest Facebook status sheds some light on her life these days:

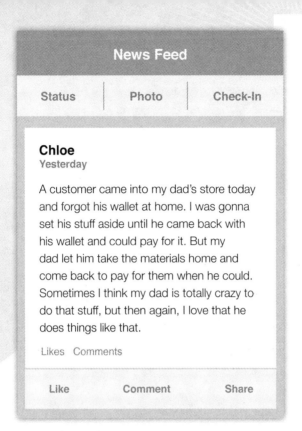

News Feed

Status | Photo | Check-In

Chloe
Yesterday

A customer came into my dad's store today and forgot his wallet at home. I was gonna set his stuff aside until he came back with his wallet and could pay for it. But my dad let him take the materials home and come back to pay for them when he could. Sometimes I think my dad is totally crazy to do that stuff, but then again, I love that he does things like that.

Likes Comments

Like   Comment   Share

While watching the news last night, Chloe saw a short segment on a local high school student who received a scholarship to a major university. The report focused on how hard this guy had worked through high school and how his hard work and commitments were now paying off. It got Chloe thinking, and before she went to sleep, she spent a few minutes writing in her journal:

Everyone seems to be going in different directions. On the news tonight there was a story about a guy who was going to Notre Dame with a full scholarship. Jeff is off and running with his engineering career. Sometimes I wonder if I'm missing out.

But I'm not those people. I'm my own person with my own priorities. I realized there are some things about me that I don't ever want to change.

I'm committed to my family.

I'm committed to honesty and integrity; my dad has taught me that.

I'm committed to living out my faith in Jesus.

I don't know a lot of things and I have a lot of unanswered questions about life, but I at least know I can stand on these three things. Wherever I go and whatever I end up doing in my life, I never want these things to change about me. I think these commitments should shape my life.

This is my framework.

IT'S IMPORTANT TO HAVE A FRAMEWORK

READY. SET. NEXT.

Regardless of what you think you will do after graduating, it's really helpful to figure out the things you want to remain committed to in your life. Identifying and articulating a few things now can really help you stand firm when things around you begin to change.

1. **What three commitments have had the biggest impact on your life so far?**

2. **What specific commitments do you want to shape the rest of your life—and why?**

3. **What kinds of people do you think could naturally or easily help you keep these commitments? How might you connect with these types of people once you finish high school?**

CHAPTER 4:

YOUR RELATIONSHIP WITH YOUR PARENTS CAN BE TRICKY

PROFILE: JOHN

Age: 18

Year: College freshman

Sport: Played baseball in high school

Parents: Divorced; dad about to get remarried

Car: Parked at his mom's house because he can't have one as a freshman

Genre of music: Still can't stand country

Paused on iTunes: Now uses Spotify

Quirk: Loves elevators

Wants to: Have parents who understand him

Pet peeve: Guys running around naked in the dorm

John wasn't sure if or where he'd end up going to college, but he's now in the middle of the spring semester of his freshman year at Oregon State University. He's been back home twice since he left for college: once for Thanksgiving and again at Christmas break. Overall, he's pretty settled into college life now. However, he is still struggling with how to talk about his life with his parents—especially his mom. It's been a topic in many text conversations with his girlfriend, Sasha…

READY.
SET.
NEXT.

YOUR RELATIONSHIP WITH YOUR PARENTS CAN BE TRICKY

John

Just got off the phone with my mom. Can you talk?

Sasha

Shoot I JUST got in class. I'll call when I'm out...is everything ok?

John

Alright. Not really, it was frustrating. Can't talk to her about anything these days.

Sasha

So sorry :-(I will pray for you right now!

John

Thx. I need to be patient. I know she loves me but sometimes it's like she doesn't care what I think because all she cares about is that I'm going to OSU.

Sasha

So sorry! I will call as soon as I can!! Hang in there!

John

K. I'm heading to library so just text when you can talk and I'll call you back.

Sasha

Perfect. Love you!

Send

At this moment in his life, John feels like he can't talk honestly to either of his parents about what's actually going on with him. Sometimes he wishes he had another older adult he could spend time with, to help him think through stuff—someone who wouldn't be biased and could just give objective advice without stressing out about how he's doing in his classes.

If only he knew how common this struggle was for college students—and how everyone else entering the first years of life after high school goes through similar struggles.

He doesn't want to admit it to most people, but he questions his parents' motives. The biggest example: Going to OSU is a massive thing for them. His parents met there and have always expected him and his brother to go there, too. It was always assumed that he and Stephan would follow in their steps, but his parents never asked John how he feels about it. They're now proud that he's attending there—but that's a big part of the problem.

John isn't completely sure of his life direction yet, but he's certain he wants to be his own person (even if he doesn't always know exactly what that means or what it'll require). Living in the shadow of his parents' expectations is really starting to wear on him.

He often wonders if he's overthinking things or making this a bigger deal than it should be. This week he reached out to his brother to talk about it. Stephan lives in another state these days, but John tries to talk with him pretty often.

John

Hey. I would've called but it's 1:40am your time. Anyway, I'm wondering if you could help me out with Mom and Dad. How did you deal with them? Sometimes I feel like all they care about is me coming to OSU like they did. Did you ever feel like that?

Stephan

Yo! Bro, I'm not sure how I did it. Just try and remind yourself of the fact that they've done a lot for us to be able to go there. I've told you this before, but now that I'm done I'm really thankful I went there. Do you want to go to a different school?

John

I don't know. Sometimes I think it would just be better to go to a community college like Sasha is. Seems like that would be much simpler. I know they worked hard to get me here, but sometimes I just feel like we are their trophies to be shown off to their friends. I don't remember them being like this with you. Maybe I was just naive to everything? Now I don't even want to talk to them about anything because they just keep telling me I need to focus on my schoolwork. As if I'm not!

Stephan

I don't know, they were pretty stressed about everything with me, too. Hang in there! I'll try to talk to them about it and see if I can get them to relax a bit.

John

Okay, thanks man. I appreciate it.

Write a reply...

Add Files   Add Photos   Reply

Talking through all this stuff with Sasha and Stephan helped John—a reminder that sometimes it's just good to get some outside opinions. John even talked a little with Sasha's dad and got some solid advice from him, too. But the best conversation was with Chris, a guy he bumped into (almost literally) in the church lobby one Sunday morning. It was crazy: John came out of the church service, went to get a donut and some coffee, and Chris—along with his wife—randomly asked if he wanted to join them for lunch. They offered to pay, so how could a broke college student say no to a couple in their 50s who were willing to buy him lunch? At first John felt a little awkward about it because he had never been approached like that by people he hadn't met before, but it ended up being a fantastic experience. It was so cool for them to invite him along.

They had a great time talking, and near the end of lunch, Chris suggested that he and John get together for coffee sometime—an awesome idea, John thought. They met a few days later at Well & Good coffeehouse, each ordered a non-fat vanilla latte, Chris paid, and they sat down in the most amazingly comfortable leather chairs next to a fireplace. John enjoyed how Chris just asked him questions—and really *listened.* It was so encouraging for John to talk with someone who was genuinely interested in what he was experiencing. He spoke honestly about his struggle with his parents, and that's when Chris said something that totally changed John's thoughts on his relationship with his parents.

After listening to John explain his perspective, Chris thought it would be helpful for John to hear a parent's point of view. "I've had some tensions with my kids, too. When they went off to college, it was hard to figure out our relationship. I crossed some boundaries with them, probably like your parents are doing with you. What I can tell you, John, is that your parents love you deeply and they probably want you to be an independent adult. But letting go is really hard as a parent, and my guess is that they're just trying to figure out how to do that, just like you're trying to figure it out. I guess my advice is this: Don't stop calling them. Keep filling them in on bits and pieces of your life. As a parent myself, I really think that's all they want. They just want to still be a part of your life."

That advice transformed the way John looked at his situation. After that conversation, John made a commitment to call his mom and his dad at least once a week just so he could tell them a few things that were going on in his life. He also tried to mention a few things about his classes, too. What he realized—especially with his mom—was that if he just took a little time out of his week to make a call, those interactions became a lot more enjoyable.

READY. SET. NEXT.

Most people's relationship with their parent(s) will change to some degree after high school. Obviously, some of us experience more or deeper change than others, but you need to expect *some* level of change. It's also important to remember that it's hard for both sides. Consider thinking through the following questions:

1. **What do your parents want for you? Think of specific times they've verbalized it—or times they've at least hinted at their hopes and desires for you.**

2. **What are a couple of things you don't feel like you can talk about with your parent(s)? What would need to change for you to feel comfortable talking about those issues or topics?**

3. **What steps can you initiate with your parent(s) to help protect your relationship with them?**

4. **Do you think being apart from your parent(s) will be freeing or hard for you? What will it be like for them?**

CHAPTER 5:

IT'S NOT EASY BEING WHO YOU ARE

PROFILE: AMY

Age: 20

Year: College sophomore

Sport: Been to one college basketball game

Parents: Married for 23 years

Car: Still sitting in front of her parents' house

Genre of music: Recently listening to indie stuff

Paused on iTunes: Arctic Monkeys

Quirk: Freezes grapes and eats them as a late-night snack

Wants to: Figure out how she fits into the world

Pet peeve: People who talk during a movie

Amy's been trying to memorize a verse from the Bible: Colossians 3:17.

¹²Put on then, as God's chosen ones, holy and beloved, compassionate hearts, kindness, humility, meekness, and patience, ¹³bearing with one another and, if one has a complaint against another, forgiving each other; as the Lord has forgiven you, so you also must forgive. ¹⁴And let the peace of Christ rule in your hearts, to which indeed you were called in one body. And be thankful. ¹⁵And let the peace of Christ rule in your hearts, to which indeed you were called in the one body. And be thankful. ¹⁶Let the word of Christ dwell in you richly, teaching and admonishing one another in all wisdom, singing psalms and hymns and spiritual songs, with thankfulness in your hearts to God. **¹⁷And whatever you do, in word or deed, do everything in the name of the Lord Jesus, giving thanks to God the Father through him.**

Deep down she wants everything in her life to reflect her faith and what she believes about Jesus, but she's really struggling. In fact, she's starting to drown in guilt for not being who she thinks she should be. She's convinced that memorizing Scripture will help her—after all, that's what everyone told her as a kid. She sees a lot of inconsistencies in her life and, frankly, it's wearing on her. She desires to be authentic, but it's not coming easily.

Last month she went to a party and had too much to drink; a friend had to take her back to her dorm. She also recently broke up with her boyfriend because they kept going too far physically, and Amy was tired of the guilt it was causing her.

She feels good about that decision, but it's left her feeling lonely again. She enjoyed having someone to hang out with all the time. She is thinking through so much stuff, yet it's as if nobody else knows—one of the toughest parts of life after high school. She keeps it all to herself. She doesn't feel like anyone else would understand, so she just continues putting on a smile and "going through the motions" so nobody recognizes what's really going on. And the fact is, she wouldn't even know what to say if someone asked her to explain it. It's sort of a twisted ball of twine in her head right now.

The guilt and questions have caused her to feel less comfortable when she attends the campus ministry, too. Amy recently journaled some questions she's been asking herself.

Life seems to be filled with a lot of unanswered questions. I often wonder if some of them are even answerable! It can be so frustrating, but I'm finding that the key for me is to make sure I'm at least trying to ask the right questions. These are some of the questions I've been asking myself...

Who am I?

Who does God say I am, and how can I possibly be that person?

Who do I want to be a part of my life?

Where do I belong?

Who do I want to become, and how can I get to that point?

What does God want me to do for work?

How do I prepare for that?

I'm starting to wonder if I'll ever find the answers.

IT'S NOT EASY BEING WHO YOU ARE

After writing those words, Amy closed her journal and set it on the floor next to her bed. She turned off the lamp and stretched out on her bed. Within minutes, she'd fallen asleep on top of her covers; she didn't even change out of her clothes.

The next morning she awoke to a familiar sound from the bathroom: her roommate's hairdryer. At first Amy was a little frustrated. Heather doesn't really seem to take her into consideration, but Amy is too nice to say anything about it. When Heather was done with her hair, she walked back out into the room and saw that Amy was awake.

"Wow, girl. Did you pass out or something? You didn't even change out of your clothes!" Heather said.

Amy smiled. "No, I was just so tired last night that I didn't care." As she got up from her bed, she threw her hair back and wrapped it up into a bun.

Her roommate said, "Yeah, no kidding. You were out cold. I tried to wake you up last night when I came home, but you didn't budge." Amy laughed.

Amy took a shower and got herself ready. She didn't have any set plans for the day, so she wanted to take advantage of the opportunity to spend some time alone. She decided to head to the student union to get some coffee and read a book for a while. She was really looking forward to getting her mind off things.

She grabbed her bag and phone. As she was walking down the hallway, she noticed she had a random text message from her old youth pastor, Ryan. She sometimes saw him at church when she was home visiting, but getting the text was a bit of a surprise.

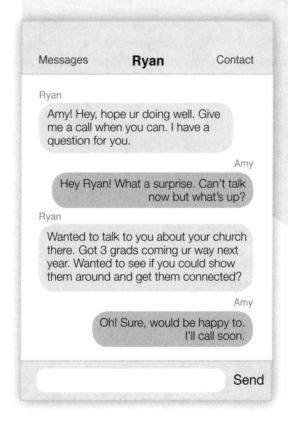

Messages · **Ryan** · Contact

Ryan
> Amy! Hey, hope ur doing well. Give me a call when you can. I have a question for you.

Amy
> Hey Ryan! What a surprise. Can't talk now but what's up?

Ryan
> Wanted to talk to you about your church there. Got 3 grads coming ur way next year. Wanted to see if you could show them around and get them connected?

Amy
> Oh! Sure, would be happy to. I'll call soon.

Send

Suddenly, Amy was in a tough position. How could she help three other people get connected? She was trying to figure out so many things herself—plus she wasn't a part of any church. She was barely even involved in the InterVarsity group on campus. This was yet another thing she had to figure out. Everyone, including her parents, assumed she was doing great, especially in her faith. But that's because she was hiding her inner turmoil.

She maintained an outward appearance of her high school identity to people at home and was too proud to let anyone in college know about her inner struggles. Her youth pastor still looked to her as a leader, which she appreciated and valued, but the truth was that she didn't even know how to lead herself right now.

Amy had to figure this stuff out but didn't know how. She wasn't the same person anymore, but without anyone to talk with about what was really going on, the feelings of loneliness frequently took over. The weight of guilt was becoming too much to carry. She definitely didn't want her parents to know how much she was struggling. So, in her mind, Ryan's close connection to her family eliminated him as a potential person to talk with, too.

That day she posted some thoughts on Instagram:

likes
amy Trying to figure out how to be where I am.
It's not easy.

IT'S NOT EASY BEING WHO YOU ARE

READY. SET. NEXT.

Being really honest about how you are doing in your faith can be difficult at times. This is especially the case for many young adults, who are examining and re-evaluating what they believe.

1. **Are you currently being honest with the people around you about how you are really doing in your faith?**

2. **What specific fears can keep you from being really honest with people?**

3. **If you don't have someone you can talk with honestly, what are a few ways you might look for and find that kind of person?**

CHAPTER 6:

IT'S HARD TO FIGURE OUT WHAT YOU WANT TO DO

PROFILE: CHLOE

Age: 19

Year: Not in school

Sport: Plays in a volleyball league

Parents: Married for 19 years

Car: Same truck, different tires

Genre of music: Country

Paused on iTunes: Taylor Swift—"22"

Quirk: Always wears mismatched socks

Wants to: Be honest

Pet peeve: When adults cuss in front of children

BLOG

HOME · ABOUT · ARCHIVES

I'm Glad

I'm glad I didn't go to college, because I still don't know what I want to do with my life. But I feel pressure to be someone different from who I am right now. All my friends are moving on, yet I'm stuck in the same place.

Sometimes I think I made a mistake by staying home after h.s.

Will things ever change?
Will I live at home forever?
How can I possibly get out on my own?
Where would I live?

Comment   Share

Chloe has been out of high school for just over a year. At first she was totally content with not "moving on." But she's starting to get restless. Her cousin Jeff is having such a great time away at school, and all but one of her friends are off to either the community college or to another college or university. When her friends call and ask how things are going, she just feels dumb.

IT'S HARD TO FIGURE OUT WHAT YOU WANT TO DO

Her routines are the same as they were a year ago, but the world seems to be passing her by.

She still loves many things about staying at home. She loves riding her horse. She loves taking the quad up the trail to the stream, where she sits and enjoys the peaceful setting. She loves spending time in the playhouse while Maria makes plastic food for her to "eat" and "drink."

Chloe loves her family, but she's about ready to move on now.

But she has no idea what she would move on to.

She's saved up about $3,000 that could pay for classes at the community college. But because she doesn't know what she wants to do or study yet, she doesn't want to spend the money right now.

While at the store one day helping her dad with some stuff, Chloe hit a breaking point as she unpacked some cleaning supplies in the storeroom. She'd been working on the project for about 30 minutes when she suddenly stopped, sat down on one of the unpacked boxes, held a bottle of cleaner with both hands in her lap, and just stared at the bottle. She felt lost and was lonely.

I'm so frustrated. Why can't I figure out what I want to do?!
Maybe I should just pick something and run with that.
But what if that is the wrong direction?
God, what do you want me to do?

These thoughts continued to run through her mind for the rest of the day. Fear of heading in the wrong direction was causing her to not run in *any* direction.

When she got home that evening she went straight into her bedroom. Her mom was cooking in the kitchen so she didn't even see Chloe come in. Chloe got to her room, sat on the floor at the foot of her bed, leaned back against the footboard, and texted her friend Julie.

READY. SET. NEXT.

IT'S HARD TO FIGURE OUT WHAT YOU WANT TO DO

Chloe

You coming home for spring break?

Julie

Chloe! Oh, no, a group of us are going down to New Orleans. I'm so excited!

Chloe

That's awesome! You doing okay otherwise?

Julie

Yeah, going great here. School is crazy hard but my roommate this year is awesome. So much better than last year! How r u?

Chloe

I'm so glad to hear that. Oh, I'm doing really good. I love being home. My dad really needs my help and I love being here with my family!

Julie

That's so awesome, Chloe. I miss home a lot. I miss going up to the stream with you! Maybe we can do that this summer!!!

Chloe

Of course! Hey, gotta run but let's talk soon! Would love to catch up more.

Julie

For sure! Love ya!

Send

READY. SET. NEXT.

Insecurity was causing Chloe to not tell the truth. Sure, a text conversation probably wasn't the best way to spill out her guts. But she didn't really want anyone else to know how she was truly doing. She didn't want to burden anyone.

"Dinner is ready!" Her mom's announcement interrupted her pensive thoughts.

Chloe got up, threw her phone on the bed, and went out into the kitchen. Once everyone was settled into their seats, Chloe's dad prayed.

Father, thank you for all that you've given us. We are so grateful for your provision. We don't deserve all this, but you have graciously given to us. Thank you so much for this food and for my wife, who always prepares our food with a loving heart. In Jesus' name, amen.

Even though her dad has prayed the same prayer every night since she was a little girl, she knows one thing: Her dad means every single word of it. Chloe respects her dad so much. He is so genuine, loving, giving, and gentle. He's such a great example of a husband who sincerely loves his wife.

In times like this, Chloe realizes how blessed she is.

But then her mom threw out a curveball. As the mashed potatoes, broccoli, rice, and chicken were being passed around the table, her mom said, "Well, I want all of you to know about something so you can be praying. Aunt Carol told me today that Jeff is going to drop out of school."

Chloe was shocked. "What?!"

"Yeah. I guess he's decided he doesn't like engineering as much as he thought he would. So, he's going to be moving back home for a little while," her mom said.

"Oh boy, what a change," her dad replied.

Chloe sat there in momentary silence and then said, "What about his scholarship? What is he going to do?"

"Well, Aunt Carol says he's probably just going to get a job until he figures out what he wants to do. His scholarship will be voided if he leaves, so..." her mom replied as she shrugged her shoulders.

Chloe sat there with wide eyes. Complete shock. Then her dad graciously said, "It's not uncommon. I read an article the other day that said most college students change their major two or three times before they graduate. And apparently, only 25 percent of college grads have a full-time job lined up when they graduate, and a huge percentage of them only got the job because they took something that was different from what they studied in college. I tell ya, it's a tough world out there."

Chloe silently finished her food.

After dinner she helped clean up the kitchen like she always did and then went back to her room. She picked up her phone and saw a notification from a tweet Julie had sent out:

Tweet

Julie
@julesbirdpdcx

Honesty isn't always the easiest thing. #truth

Reply

Chloe started to wonder if Julie was actually doing as well as she implied in their text conversation…

READY. SET. NEXT.

Determining what you want to do in life can be difficult. Very few people have it nailed down in their first couple of years after finishing high school—and some people are still trying to figure it out many years after graduating! Here are some questions to consider:

1. **Are you ready for your life direction to change a few times? Why or why not?**

2. **If your life direction does change, what will it take to be honest about it with other people?**

3. **Who in your life can help you process through your life direction? If you don't have someone, what person could you ask to be that "outside voice" in your life through your first few years after high school?**

CHAPTER 7:

OTHER PEOPLE WILL PLAY A HUGE ROLE IN YOUR LIFE

PROFILE: JOHN

Age: 20

Year: College junior

Sport: Plays Ultimate Frisbee every once in a while

Parents: Mom still single; dad now remarried

Car: Parked in lot A at OSU; doesn't drive it much

Genre of music: Getting interested in classic rock

Paused on iTunes: Been listening to the Journey station on Spotify

Quirk: Fascinated by airplanes

Wants to: Become strategic about friendships

Pet peeve: Roommates leaving dirty dishes in the sink

John

Hey Larry, my name is John Owen and I'm friends with Chris Newman. Chris has mentored me for about two years now. We both go to Horizon Church. Anyway, he's told me a little about how you consult with small-business owners. I'm currently finishing up my junior year at OSU and was wondering if you would be up for a cup of coffee sometime. I've been working on a business plan, and if you would be willing, I'd love to get any thoughts you have on it. It's rough and this is the first time I've ever done one, so I'd appreciate any help you could give me.

Thanks and hope to hear from you soon,

John

Larry

Hey John! Yeah, Chris has told me a bit about you. Sure, I'd love to connect and help any way I can. I'm currently out of town, but I fly back on Friday. Would you be able to connect next Tuesday or Wednesday afternoon?

Looking forward to it,

Larry

Write a reply...

Add Files   Add Photos   Reply

In recent months, John has been learning an important fact of life: People know other people. That may sound obvious, but it's an essential concept in adulthood. John's relationship with Chris has been much more helpful and encouraging than he could ever have imagined. Being connected to a local church like Horizon also has paid off for John. Not only has he built friendships that help him feel comfortable at Horizon now, but he also has grown in his faith more than he thought he could. His relationship with Chris has been a critical piece for this growth, and that friendship has opened doors to connect with some other followers of Christ, too.

One of the most helpful things for John has been his interaction with older married couples. Because his parents divorced when he was young, he's never really seen what a Christlike marriage looks like—at least, not firsthand or close-up. But the connections he's developed with people at church have shown him a few things he will never forget: (1) Nobody is perfect and every marriage has its own struggles, (2) people can choose to remain committed to working through challenges or struggles in a marriage, and (3) marriage can be a wonderful thing.

This exposure has given him a lot of hope for his relationship with his girlfriend, Sasha. She finished up two years of community college and is now attending OSU, just like John. They were able to keep their long-distance relationship going, but it wasn't always easy. They endured some struggles and even broke things off a couple of times, but now their relationship is going strong.

Sasha has gotten involved at Horizon Church, too. She meets with Chris' wife, Karyn, for coffee about twice a month. And Sasha and John have dinner at Chris and Karyn's house at least once a week—often enough that they know where all the dishes in the kitchen belong. Having this connection has proven to be a huge blessing. Sasha highly respects her parents, but seeing another marriage close-up has been very enlightening, and watching John grow so much because of these connections has been powerfully affirming.

READY. SET. NEXT.

OTHER PEOPLE WILL PLAY A HUGE ROLE IN YOUR LIFE

John

Dude, how did you meet your business partner?

Stephan

Met at OSU. Why?

John

Just wondering. How did you meet?

Stephan

Had a couple classes w him and we were in same small group through Cru.

John

Got it.

Stephan

You still involved at that church?

John

Yep

Stephan

Getting some good friends?

John

Yeah getting to know a few people pretty good actually

Stephan

Still hanging out w/ that older guy?

John

Sasha and I go over there for dinner a lot with him and his wife.

Stephan

That's cool. Wish I had that in college! Make sure you connect with other students too!

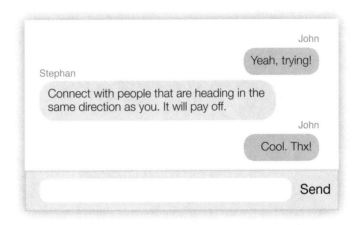

John

Yeah, trying!

Stephan

Connect with people that are heading in the same direction as you. It will pay off.

John

Cool. Thx!

Send

John had a lot of things in place. But the closer he got to his senior year, the more he realized that he didn't really know many students at school. Sure, he had friends, but he hadn't developed many friendships with people who were committed to the same things as he was. His friends were all really cool people that he loved spending time with, but he started to think that it might be good to get a little more intentional about the people he hung out with most.

John pulled out his Moleskine and wrote down some thoughts:

I'm realizing that I need to make some more friends. I want to meet more people and get to know some other Christians who love some of the same things I love. I kind of wish I had done that earlier.

2 things to do before summer:
(1) Connect with Professor Oswald to get more advice on doing well during my final year.
(2) Hang with Lucas more. It would be cool to work with him someday.

2 things to talk to Sasha about:
(1) Getting involved in the college group a little more next year.
(2) Figuring out how to connect our groups of friends.

READY. SET. NEXT.

With your commitments in mind and with an understanding of the powerful role relationships can play in your life, consider these questions:

1. **What types of people do you want to surround yourself with during your first few years after high school? Why?**

2. **What kinds of places or groups could be good starting points to begin some of these relationships?**

3. **What are some things—or some types of people—you want to limit connection with because you feel like they may not help you in your commitments?**

OTHER PEOPLE WILL PLAY A HUGE ROLE IN YOUR LIFE

CHAPTER 8:

TO FIND YOURSELF, YOU NEED MORE THAN A MIRROR

PROFILE: AMY

Age: 21

Year: End of sophomore year in college

Sport: Still has attended just one basketball game

Parents: Married for 24 years

Car: Her mom has started driving it while Amy is at school

Genre of music: Hooked on indie music

Paused on iTunes: Future of Forestry— "Hills of Indigo Blue"

Quirk: Is a master at the Rubik's Cube

Wants to: Be where she is

Pet peeve: People who talk loud on their cell phones in public places

Around 10:30 p.m. one Wednesday night, Amy found herself studying in the library—not her ideal place, but she had to prepare for a test coming up that Friday. As she sat there cramming her brain with all kinds of details about European literature, a guy came and sat next to her. Amy glanced over and noticed he needed some more room at the table, so she graciously moved her bag to the other side of her chair and then shifted her books over a bit to the left to give him more space. She was really focused on her work and was wearing headphones, so she didn't even acknowledge the guy directly. She just kept studying.

About a half-hour later, she glanced away from her own books and papers, and noticed the title of a book the guy had out: *Identity Crisis*. Amy paused, and looked at the book. After a moment, she tapped the guy on the shoulder, and he took off his own headphones to see what she wanted.

"Hey, sorry to bother you, but what class is that book for?"

"Psychology," he said.

"Is the book any good?" Amy asked.

"Not sure. I haven't read it yet. But I'm supposed to write a reflection paper on it by tomorrow," the guy said as he chuckled.

Amy laughed and then said, "OK, well, good luck with that."

The library was about to close, so she packed up her things and started walking back to her room. Her dorm was just across the quad, but it felt like a mile away. Her mind was racing a thousand miles an hour. For the last year or so, Amy had been thinking through who she is and where she belonged. Life had gotten busy, she dated a guy for a while, and her studies seemed like they were getting more and more intense. She had slowly allowed the busyness of college life to squeeze out what was once truly important to her.

You could say she was just kind of floating through life. During this walk back to her dorm, it hit her: She had stopped a critical thought process. Maybe it was a self-defense thing. Maybe it was just too stressful so she had just compartmentalized it and decided to have some fun. Or maybe she was just overthinking it.

She finally made it to her room, set down her bag, took off her shoes, pulled out her laptop, and opened her Facebook account. She just wanted to get her mind off all this. But one of her friends had posted a status that stood out like a bright orange T-shirt on a barista would.

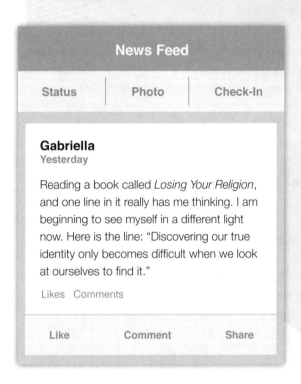

News Feed

| Status | Photo | Check-In |

Gabriella
Yesterday

Reading a book called *Losing Your Religion*, and one line in it really has me thinking. I am beginning to see myself in a different light now. Here is the line: "Discovering our true identity only becomes difficult when we look at ourselves to find it."

Likes   Comments

| Like | Comment | Share |

Amy saw that one person had commented on the post:

| Like | Comment | Share |

Huh? That doesn't make ANY sense.

TO FIND YOURSELF, YOU NEED MORE THAN A MIRROR

Gabriella had replied to the comment with a helpful clarification:

Like	Comment	Share

The whole thought is if we want to figure out who we are as individuals, we have to look to Jesus. It's a Christian book. So the point of the author is that God defines us by what Jesus has done for us and not by what we have done, are doing, or will do. It really has me thinking about how I identify myself.

Needless to say, this struck a chord with Amy. This was exactly what she'd been thinking about, and now it seemed like all these things were popping out of nowhere. She couldn't handle it. It was too intense. She shut her computer, set it on her desk, and then grabbed the *Modern Europe Literature* book she needed to read for Friday's test. She didn't have time to think about all this identity stuff. She had to study.

Two weeks later, Amy was sitting in the room where her InterVarsity group met. She hadn't been to the group for a while but decided to go this night. They were in the middle of a series called "Questions," which addressed some big questions of life that people ask. It was right up her alley.

Different leaders spoke for three minutes each about the questions they'd been asking lately and what they were learning by asking them. The third student leader to share said something that really caught Amy's attention:

"I've been asking the question, 'Who am I?' So, over the past couple of years I have been trying to figure that out. It's a good question to ask, but I'm learning that I have to ask an entirely different question to find the answer. I think the better question to ask is, 'Who does God say I am?' That's the question I would encourage you to ask yourself tonight. It's by asking *that* question that I've discovered who I really am. I just needed to take the focus off myself to find it."

Amy was totally freaking out—internally, of course. She's too reserved to show too much on the outside. But it felt like everything in her life was saying the same thing. She was blown away and, honestly, a little spooked. It was almost as if God was *forcing* her to think through this stuff. She could no longer ignore it. She started to tear up, so when the closing music started she got up and slipped out before anyone could see her.

It was a moment of both brokenness and freedom.

She got back to her dorm room and wrote a poem and some thoughts in her journal.

I can no longer run from this

I will no longer fight it with clinched fists

I am open to what's to come

Discovering myself in what he has done

I've already won

Finding myself by looking to God's Son

I've allowed my surroundings to define me, and it's caused me a lot of confusion. I don't need to figure out who I am because God has already told me. I just need to embrace that.

I am God's child. That's it. It's that simple.

READY. SET. NEXT.

The trick to life after high school is to be who you are, wherever you are. So many high school students are obsessed with asking God what he wants them to do when they graduate. But the key is to strive to be who you are, now. Faithfulness today is more important than obsessing over what God might do with you and through you in the future.

1.   **Think about who God says you are, right now—what is most exciting about that, and what is most intimidating? Why?**

2.   **What is your response to the truth that God views you through what Jesus has done and NOT through the things you do?**

3.   **Read 2 Corinthians 5:14-20. Who does this passage say you are? What do you find most challenging about this Scripture, and why?**

TO FIND YOURSELF, YOU NEED MORE THAN A MIRROR

CHAPTER 9:

MONEY IS ALWAYS SOMETHING TO CONSIDER

PROFILE: CHLOE

Age: 21

Year: First year at nursing school

Sport: Still playing in volleyball league

Parents: Married for 21 years

Car: Looking to buy a new car—getting a little tired of driving a truck

Genre of music: Country

Paused on iTunes: George Strait —*Greatest Hits, Vol. 2*

Quirk: Craves Swedish Fish gummy candy

Wants to: Have a meaningful career

Pet peeve: People who write on dirty windshields

Messages **Julie** Contact

Julie
Hey! Still up for lunch?

Chloe
You know it! Can't wait to see you and catch up! Been TOO LONG!

Julie
Great. Where do you wanna meet?

Chloe
Joe's?

Julie
Wow, haven't been there in forever. I could use a chocolate shake! It will be great to see Joe too...What time?

Chloe
Yeah, haven't been there in a long time either...and I live here! Will noon work?

Julie
Perfect! Can't wait. See you then & there.

Chloe
Awesome!

Send

Chloe was excited to see Julie, who had wrapped up her junior year at college and was home for about a month. She was working at a flower shop next to her campus, so she couldn't spend the

MONEY IS ALWAYS SOMETHING TO CONSIDER

entire summer at home—even though she probably would've enjoyed that. Chloe and Julie hadn't hung out in over a year, so they were excited to catch up on life.

The two friends grew up together: Julie's parents own a farm up the road from Chloe's family, so they'd been around each other all the time. It seemed like they were in all the same classes through junior high and high school, and their families still go to the same church. They have a lot of history.

Chloe got to Joe's a little early. Joe's is a little place with only nine seats in it. Joe is 67 and has run the restaurant for almost five decades, but he still does all the cooking. His wife works the cash register, and their oldest son, Joseph, works there, too. The place is really known for its Southern-style breakfast foods, but the menu also features hamburgers and shakes. And they have the best french fries Chloe has ever tasted. Joe uses a special seasoning that he makes especially for the fries—and he refuses to tell anyone what it is.

Chloe walked in, said hi to Joe, and grabbed one of the three tables. Julie came in a few minutes later, and Joe was excited as soon as he saw her. "JULIE! Oh boy, it is sooo good to see you!" Joe came from behind the bar to give her a hug. Julie was excited to see him, too. She used to eat there with her family a few times a month. She briefly updated Joe and his wife, Madalene, on how she was doing and how school was going. Then she hugged Chloe and sat down. They quickly ordered their favorite items from the menu and started chatting.

They caught up on how things were going and what the next phase of life would be like. Chloe still had about two more years of nursing school left. She had finally determined that this was what she wanted to do, she had saved up enough money, and she had gotten into the program at the community college. Nursing was one of the bigger programs at the school and was very well-respected around her county. Chloe had saved up enough money to pay for the first two years and was still working while in school so she could pay for the last year.

Julie's story was quite different because of going away to a university right after high school. In many ways, this was a great experience and she was glad she did it. She'll graduate with a degree in social work and hopes to work with youth. She has a real heart for kids in juvenile detention centers, so she's been looking into what that would be like.

Unfortunately, she's financed most of her education with loans and doesn't know how she's going to pay them back. Her student loan payment will be about $600 a month. She originally wanted to be a pre-med student and go on to become a pediatric doctor, but that all changed. Her new career path won't pay as much money as being a doctor, so paying back those loans is going to be tough.

Her dilemma is a stressful one—and a common one for many college graduates. She loves college, but now she faces the long-term experience of paying for it. She wonders if it was worth it. She looks to Chloe and is envious because Chloe took a different route. Chloe didn't go to school the first three years, but when she

MONEY IS ALWAYS SOMETHING TO CONSIDER

graduates she won't have to pay back anything. Julie has been attending school for three years, but when she graduates she'll have to make big payments for 15 years.

After leaving Joe's, Chloe and Julie went back to Chloe's house, hopped on the quad, and went up to the stream. They hung out the rest of the day and reminisced about old times as kids. They laughed a ton, remembering all the fun things they did as little girls. It was a wonderful time for both of them. It was like they had never left each other.

Julie stayed for dinner, then went home. Later that night, around 11:30 p.m., Chloe journaled.

I'm feeling so blessed right now. Thank you, God, for giving me patience and contentment these past few years. It has been hard at times, but you've always been there.

I feel bad for Julie. I don't know what she's going to do. Please help her through this financial burden. I trust you have her where you want her, but give her peace. I'm not sure if it's wrong to pray for or not, but God, please give her a job that pays well when she graduates.

I'm at peace today. I just want to work hard like my dad has always taught me. Even though it's been tough at times, I'm thankful I've stuck to my values and priorities.

I'm still committed to (and thankful for) my family.

I'm committed to honesty and integrity.

I'm committed to living out my faith in Jesus.

MONEY IS ALWAYS SOMETHING TO CONSIDER

READY. SET. NEXT.

Too often people take out loans for their education without really thinking through the implications for their lives down the road. Getting loans could be the way to go for you, but it might only be the easiest way. It's worth thinking about the *best* way versus just the *easiest* way, so consider the following questions:

1. **How are you planning to pay for college or for vocational training?**

2. **What might paying back a loan mean for you, practically? What sorts of things will you need to give up in order to make those monthly payments?**

3. **What are some ways you could get through college or training without much—if any—debt? How might those decisions also help you avoid debt later in adulthood?**

CHAPTER 10:

PURSUE GOD'S WILL FOR YOUR LIFE

PROFILE: JOHN

Age: 21

Year: College senior

Sport: Has gone to two OSU football games

Parents: Has talked with his stepmom just three times

Car: Parked in the only spot his apartment complex gives him

Genre of music: Sold on classic rock

Paused on iTunes: Podcast of his pastor

Quirk: Fascinated by airplanes

Wants to: Figure out what God wants him to do

Pet peeve: Guys who shave their arms

Over the past two weeks, John has seen some tweets from friends that are causing him to become a little insecure:

Discover

Nick @wordynick
Been praying about getting an interview w/a magazine and JUST got an email from them. BOOM!

Alicia @alicia_wins
Interview went great! Can't wait to see what God does. #GoodToBeWhereGodWantsYou

Sydney @sosaidsyd
Job interview at 2. My hair is really red. Not sure they'll like it.

Xavier @mogulinthemaking
Interview went great! Got the job on the spot! But the guy kept looking at my beard. Might have to shave it. Yikes.

John's always been really confident about his direction in life, but now he's not so sure. He keeps hearing people talk about how 75 percent of college students don't step right into a full-time job after they graduate. He still wants to start his own business and is working on that plan, but he also has some bills to pay. He is feeling the pressure to get some kind of job soon. His business degree might help, and he has developed some good connections through school, but he doesn't have anything set right now. He has sent out some résumés but hasn't heard anything back yet.

But the underlying tension is about something more, something deeper than just a job. He is wondering what God wants him to do with his life. That's a much more intense question to wrestle with and attempt to answer. Yeah, he needs to get a job, but he wants his work to be *more than just a job.* He wants to do what God wants him to do, what God created him to do. But, well, he doesn't have any answers yet.

He's talked to his mentor, Chris, about this a bit and even had a couple of conversations with his dad, but one night he decided to email his college pastor. They've gotten to know each other pretty well over the last few months, and John has grown to trust and appreciate him. John was just hoping to get some thoughts from a faith perspective—and he also wasn't sure he was asking the right questions. His pastor emailed him back and they set up a time to meet the next morning at a nearby Panera.

That morning, John got a cinnamon crunch bagel, toasted, with cream cheese—his favorite, but he usually can't afford it. But this time his pastor, Mark, paid for it. Can't go wrong with that.

As they sat in a small booth away from the clangs and chatter of the café's kitchen, John gave Mark all the details on his struggle and questions. That's when the fresh perspective he was hoping for started to come in.

Mark asked a question that threw John back a bit at first: "Do you think God cares about what you do for a living?"

Of course God cares about what I do for a living, John thought to himself.

But that's not what he said. Instead, John replied, "Well, I think so; am I wrong in thinking that?" Mark looked back at him and simply said, "Let me ask you a little different question: Do you think God sees a difference in you as a person if you are a business owner or a third-grade teacher?"

That really got John thinking. He'd always tied his identity to his vocational pursuits so closely that he never considered what God thought about them—or what God thought about him in midst of those pursuits. John had always had a sense of pride and identity in what he was *going* to be doing for a living.

Mark continued: "Look, I appreciate that you are thinking through what God wants you to do. You'll figure something out, I'm sure. But the real question is this: Who does God want you to be?"

John replied, "I guess I've never really looked at my career like that before."

PURSUE GOD'S WILL FOR YOUR LIFE

Mark finished his thought by saying, "I'd encourage you to think a little differently about this. Sure, you need to find a job. But the issue isn't really figuring out what God wants you to do as much as it is how you can be like Jesus in everything you do—whatever that is. Does that make sense?"

It made perfect sense to John.

Later that day he told Sasha about his conversation with Mark, and those thoughts challenged and encouraged her, too. Like John, she'd never really thought about it like that before. The pressure to get a job was still there, but the focus was entirely different. About 15 minutes into the conversation, Sasha remembered something she had journaled a few days earlier.

She usually didn't share her journal with anyone, not even John, but she pulled it out and turned to a page where she had written something in huge letters across the top of a page:

GOD LOOKS AT ME AND SEES JESUS
Romans 8 : 1

Later that night, John was sitting in the middle of his bed, surrounded by a few books from his 19th century U.S. history class. He was working on his laptop, trying to get a paper written. But he couldn't concentrate on the assignment. He just sat there staring at the blank wall. His thinking was totally changing about his job pursuits.

He noticed a napkin on the nightstand behind him and to the right. He lay back on his bed, reached out, snagged the napkin, and then sat back up. He closed his laptop so it would be a solid writing surface. He removed a pen from the binding of one of his books and started writing on the napkin:

"I am not what I do."

Right below that he wrote, "God's will: to make me more like Jesus."

He then he wrote, "FREEDOM!" and underlined it—three times.

He put the napkin next to him on the bed. He flopped back, with his head landing on his pillow, and he stared at the ceiling. A smile slowly spread across his face.

That napkin symbolized the fork in the road for his life. That night was when he realized that God was going to do amazing things in him, regardless of what he was going to do for a living. He simply had to be who God was making him to be, in whatever God gave him to do.

READY. SET. NEXT.

Regardless of how confident or anxious you feel about your direction in life, you can experience incredible freedom as you more clearly understand what it means to pursue God's will. Consider these questions:

1. **If you ever feel stressed trying to figure out what God wants you to do with the rest of your life, what's most stressful? If you don't feel that stress, what advice might you offer to someone who does experience it?**

2. **What do you think about the idea that, ultimately, God's will is that you would simply be like Jesus—regardless of what you do for work?**

3. **Do you think God cares what you do for a living? Why or why not?**

4. **If you're faithful to who you are today, how can that help you recognize or understand what God wants to reveal about the rest of your life?**

CHAPTER 11:

ALWAYS KEEP THE BIG PICTURE IN MIND

PROFILE: AMY

Age: 23

Year: College senior

Sport: Now has been to three basketball games

Parents: Married for 26 years

Car: She has it now, but the heater broke, so that's a bummer

Genre of music: Kind of digging folk/rock stuff now

Paused on iTunes: Hunter Parrish—"Heart of Stone"

Quirk: Always carries two kinds of gum in her purse

Wants to: Help others through hard times

Pet peeve: Baggy jeans

Rearview Mirror Regrets

My dreams of what my life would look like during and after college haven't all come true.

In two months I will graduate from college. I used to think of college as a hoop I had to jump through to reach the other side. The side of freedom. Independence. The side where I would be confidently engaged in all God had for me.

Now I'm driving this car called "college" to its end destination, and I'm finding my reality to be very different from what I once dreamed. I look back in the rearview mirror and see a few things I would do differently. So I thought for this post, I would just list out what that rearview mirror reveals about this road I've traveled.

1. I regret being so prideful and not letting people into my struggles my freshman and sophomore years. Talking through things with someone would've been so nice.

2. I wish the person that people saw me as being was actually the person that looked outside of my eyes. I've grown a lot now, but it's been a long road.

3. I realize how much I've missed out by not being a part of a church. I've really enjoyed the campus ministry, but now I don't even know where to start when it comes to finding a church.

But I also see a bigger picture. It's like one of those prints that, when you look at it up close, you only see a mess of pen strokes, but then you step away and see the picture each pen stroke created. It's beautiful when you step back and examine it.

When I step back I see how God was a part of my story. But looking forward I see how I get to be a part of his story.

That's the biggest lesson I want to pass on.

Comment   Share

Amy's been doing really well lately. She not only understands that God identifies her as his child, but she's also starting to understand what that means. In this way, she has really grown a lot in her faith. She's even become a leader in the campus ministry and for the last year has mentored one of the three girls her youth pastor talked to her about a couple of years ago.

It's not like she has all the answers. Who does?! But she has been able to help younger girls ask some of the right questions.

Who does God say I am?
What can I do to be that person at school, today?
How can I help as many people as possible understand who God is?

You see, Amy went through a process that every young adult faces at some level or another. Now she wants to help others who are struggling to find out who they are. She knows firsthand the thoughts, questions, and fears that young adults go through. Nobody told her all those things were normal in this season of life, but now she sees it in everyone. And she wants to help.

The biggest lesson she's learned is that God brought her to this college—not just so she would get a degree, but so God could teach her a lot. A lot about herself. A lot about him. And a lot about what it means to live out her faith wherever she is. She recently got a text from Hope, the girl she is mentoring:

Hope

> Okay, so, I'm in class but can't concentrate. This prof is so boring. Wondering if we can hang out tomorrow?

Amy

> Oh, I would love to but I can't tomorrow. Maybe the next day? What's up?

Hope

> K. I was thinking about our convo last week and the fact that you will be leaving in 2 months. I have a couple questions.

Amy

> Oh, yeah, would love to hang out. What questions do you have?

Hope

> We can talk more, but for now maybe u could tell me 1 thing I should keep in mind the next two yrs of school. Tryin to just stay focused.

Amy

> Oh, great question. Let me think...

> Keep Jesus the main thing of everything. I used to try to see how he fit into everything else. That's where I got really confused. Now I ask myself how this college will be impacted by my faith, not how my faith will be impacted by college. That make sense?

Hope

> Oh wow. Yeah, I get it but that's deeper than I thought :-P

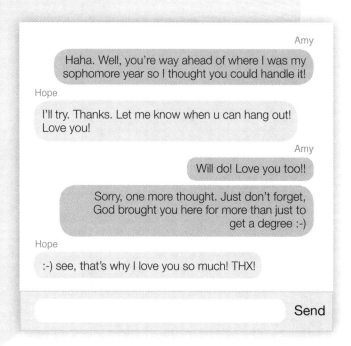

Amy

Haha. Well, you're way ahead of where I was my sophomore year so I thought you could handle it!

Hope

I'll try. Thanks. Let me know when u can hang out! Love you!

Amy

Will do! Love you too!!

Sorry, one more thought. Just don't forget, God brought you here for more than just to get a degree :-)

Hope

:-) see, that's why I love you so much! THX!

Send

The next day Amy was busy: class all morning, work from noon to 6, and then a leadership meeting for her campus ministry that lasted until 10 p.m. She got back to her room around 10:30, read for a bit, scrolled through her Twitter feed, and then checked Facebook. She spent most of her time checking out some pictures a friend had posted from a recent trip. Amy was just about to close her computer when she refreshed her page one last time. That's when she saw a post from Hope.

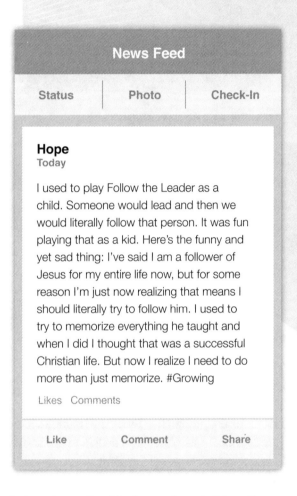

News Feed

| Status | Photo | Check-In |

Hope
Today

I used to play Follow the Leader as a child. Someone would lead and then we would literally follow that person. It was fun playing that as a kid. Here's the funny and yet sad thing: I've said I am a follower of Jesus for my entire life now, but for some reason I'm just now realizing that means I should literally try to follow him. I used to try to memorize everything he taught and when I did I thought that was a successful Christian life. But now I realize I need to do more than just memorize. #Growing

Likes Comments

Like   Comment   Share

Amy smiled as she realized that even though this college experience was hard for her in many ways, it was proving to be worth it. She didn't know what she would be doing after graduation, but she could leave college with a lot of peace.

She had grown a lot and had really tried to make the most of her final two years.

She picked up her phone, opened her Twitter app again, and sent a tweet:

Tweet

Amy
@faithfulames

In many ways I'm still lost. But in every way I'm grateful. #TheJourney

Reply

READY. SET. NEXT.

If you want to do more than just "keep" your faith after graduating from high school, consider the following questions:

1. What role do you see your faith playing in your pursuit of getting a degree or preparing for a career?

2. Think about the specific plan that seems to be unfolding for your life right after high school—why do you think God is leading you along that path?

3. Think of one person who seems to keep Jesus the main thing of everything he or she does—how could you connect with that person and learn from him or her?

4. What questions could you ask someone older than you in order to gain helpful tips for navigating life after high school?

TIPS AND THOUGHTS YOU MAY COME BACK TO

(SOME FINAL WORDS)

FAITH

◊ Write out at least five things you never want to change about you.

◊ Answer the question, "Why am I pursuing this specific path after high school?" Motivations matter to God.

◊ Turn off your cell phone every once in a while and just go for a walk. You'll find yourself thinking about things that actually matter.

◊ Money is a means to join in God's mission of reconciling the world to himself through Jesus. Unfortunately, it also can be a means of selfishness. Choose the former. You won't regret it.

◊ Sit down with at least three people who've been out of high school for a couple of years, and ask them about their experiences thus far. How do their experiences compare to your expectations?

◊ You will never have all your questions about God answered. So don't let unanswered questions consume your thoughts. Operate on what you DO know.

◊ Try to read two or three chapters in your Bible each week. Setting too high of a goal (such as reading three chapters each day) will usually set you up for failure.

◊ Pray as you walk to class. This can be more helpful than trying to set aside a separate time each day to get away and pray. Things always seem to come up that change your schedule. But if you're in college, you will always have to spend at least a few minutes walking to class.

◊ Be faithful with where you are today. If you head to college, doing your class work is the work God has for you right now. God will let you know what work he has for you after college, later. Make sure you are faithful with what God is giving you today.

◊ The more you think about what you want tomorrow to be like, the less content you will be with where you are today. Set goals, but stay focused.

◊ Get to know adults in a church. Serve in some capacity alongside adults. When you find a person, a couple, or a family that you really like, get to know where all the dishes belong in their kitchen.

RELATIONSHIPS

◊ Ask one adult who you already trust if they would be up for a monthly phone conversation.

◊ Don't try to find the right spouse. Instead, work on becoming the right one for someone else.

◊ Your parents love you and have invested the last 18 years of their lives into you. Indulge them from time to time with a phone call. Pretty sure they deserve that.

◊ Get connected to a church near your school as soon as possible. Ask your youth pastor to help you find a church.

◊ It can be hard to stay connected to people from high school if you're away at college or in the military. Pick two or three friends and talk from time to time—through phone calls, text messages, or social media.

◊ If you go home on the weekends too much, you will miss out on a lot of relational connections at school. Wade through the boring days— that's when you might meet your best friend.

◊ Have fun, but don't just hang out with people who are "fun." Hang out with people you can see becoming your really good friends.

◊ You have two ears and one mouth, which is an intelligent design. Listen more than you speak. It will pay off in relationships.

◊ Hang out with people from other cultures as much as possible. Ask them about their perceptions of your culture. You will learn more than you ever imagined.

PRACTICAL LIVING

◊ If you live in a dorm, wear flip-flops in the shower. Always.

◊ Pack the clothes you will need for college. And then take half that amount.

◊ Get involved with things on campus—even if you're a commuter student or still live at home with your family while attending school. Social productivity is good for your soul.

◊ Think. Use discernment. Just because you can do something doesn't mean you should. You'll come back to this one almost weekly.

◊ If you live in a dorm, there is always someone who walks through the hallways naked. Don't be that person.

◊ Get a flu shot yearly. When you live in a communal place, it's easy to catch what other people have—whether or not they try to throw it to you.

◊ Drying your pants (without washing them first) doesn't mean they're clean. Even if you put in a dryer sheet.

◊ If you can see the dirt ring where you lay down in your sheets, you've waited too long to wash them.

◊ The more underwear and socks you bring, the less laundry you will need to do.

◊ You'll hear about a lot of free activities on campus, so take advantage of them from time to time.

◊ Time management isn't usually the typical college student's strength. It could be helpful to use a calendar.

◊ Caffeine is likely going to be a necessity, but stay away from energy drinks. That will help you avoid weight gain and kidney stones. Coffee and tea are better. Moderation is good.

◊ Get a bike. The campus will become a lot smaller.

◊ Think about the experience you will face after college when you have to pay back all your loans, and then ask yourself, "Is that 15-year experience worth the four-year experience?" It may be, but make sure you answer the question honestly.

CLASSES

◊ If you're not a morning person, DO NOT schedule early-morning classes. You won't go.

◊ Take one extra class each term. If you really want to figure out what it's like to work 40+ hours a week, you'll need to take an extra class.

◊ Studying is like laundry. It's easier in smaller, less frequent loads.

◊ Too much socializing will equal poor grades. Everything in moderation.

◊ Go to the actual classes. Use the online ones as review.

◊ Keep study groups smaller—no more than five people. Three (including you) is ideal. More than that and it just becomes a social club.

◊ Even if you feel like your brains are oozing out of your ear or if stabbing yourself in the eye with a pencil seems better than listening to another word from your professor, stay until the end of the class. Professors often wait until the end of class to give out important information.

◊ Make the most of "wasted class time." Let's face it, sometimes class is boring—especially when the professor is droning on about some ambiguous subject or just reading the notes you already have. Sit in the back, do some homework for another class, and pop up your head every once in a while to listen to what's being said.

◊ You won't remember most of what you learn in class, but the discipline you learn to get things done in a timely fashion will impact the rest of your life. You will thank me for that later. (Seriously.)

◊ Pick a major, but hold it loosely. Most people who land a job after college usually get one outside of their major.

◊ If getting a college education were all it took to prepare you for a career, companies wouldn't have training programs. Stay humble.